On This Day

Let Happiness Seek You!

Printed in the United States of America

First Printing, 2015

Cover and book design by Kerrie Flanagan

ISBN: 978-0-9968709-0-0

To my mother Virginia

and

To my son Brett

my Before and After:

I am blessed.

On This Day

These messages have given me purpose and direction for turning the page on each new day.

My passion for the written word, whether it be to express love or loss, hope or healing, faith or freedom, has given me a focus and a mission. Sharing my passion is the goal of this collection which began in 1993.

Each year, the message has a universal tone, but in fact was very specific to private events in my life. In sharing the letters with family, friends, co-workers, and neighbors, I learned how much we humans have in common with each other, how we each are on our own quest, spoken and unspoken goals evolving inside and outside of our control and even our awareness.

On This Day has been a gift to myself, and with the encouragement of many of the recipients of these missives, my joy is to share with you.

~Jane Thrash

On this day the abundance of joy surrounds us—

abundance of thought, opportunity, interaction, support.

Count this day immediately as a success—

the gift of time cannot be purchased.

View this day as an opportunity waiting to become a memory—

hoping to be.

Accept this day, the limits of which are only—

in the time we have to share our own good self.

Remember this day, but only this moment—

to act, to believe, to be.

Say "YES" to this day, to the inevitable fact that—

we will have to suffer losses, endure changes, and become a new soul as a result.

Learn from this day: the patience of water, waiting—

for the appropriate time to be transformed into the appropriate form.

Listen to this day, asking only for—

your authenticity, the joy of knowing who you are.

Omit judgment, illuminate your potential, find your song and sing it with

all your heart.

On this day.

...the patience of water, waiting.

3

Celebrate the new day!

Celebrate the gift of fate

that we are witness to this point of reference,

this marker in the inevitable march of time.

Celebrate the infinite choices...

--the clean slate

--the new beginning

--the happy ending

Celebrate the wonderful intangibles that identify us...

--our honor

--our spirituality

--our trust

--our hope

--our soulfulness

We are by chance the stewards of each new day...

It is not by chance that we make each day count!

the clean slate, the new beginning, the happy ending

May you be blessed with seeking what you will ultimately find:

Finding the harmony in the moments of your daily life,

Living the journey with purpose and resolve,

Resolving to make your world a better place,

Placing emphasis on the gifts you have already been given,

Giving always more than you take,

Taking time to reflect and to appreciate that

You may be blessed with seeking what you have already found.

...living the journey with purpose and resolve.

May the journey continue

and we not forget the lessons offered.

May we each facilitate

the successful days of others

through compassion and contribution

of whatever our special skills might be,

or become...

May we become vested in our commitments

beyond our natural energies

as the challenges unfold...

not waiting, but seeking...

May the path you choose be filled with your light as a beacon to those

who may choose to follow.

Each one becoming....

May the gifts of the new day be gifts of peace.

not waiting, but seeking   each one becoming

In the quiet of a winter morning,

plan your journey...

Travel into the bigger picture of Life.

Create your vehicle with efficiency and forethought.

Design your highway with

marked milestones of support.

Take JOY with you every day.

Take PROMISE too, promise of what you will do.

Invite HOPE to your journey,

Seek SOLACE along your way.

Find PEACE.

Share it all.

Joy Hope Promise Solace Peace

Travel well, into the new day.

Travel into the
bigger picture of life,
with marked
milestones of support.

As the tapestry of your day becomes the tapestry of your life,

Strive to seek the experiences, offering challenges to both the mind and body,

demonstrating the reward of effort and commitment.

Let the risk become its own reward as you leave your comfort zone

seeking new horizons.

Embrace the spirit of the new day with the same boundless energy with

which it arrives.

Choose your battles.

Battle your choices.

Doubt not that you will demonstrate exactly the capabilities of your chosen mindset.

Patiently seek the joy in the gift of each day,

Remembering the best gifts you give year round have

no cost, no deadline, no expiration.

They are TRUST and HOPE,

Find your place.

Choose your destination.

Let Happiness seek YOU.

...seeking new horizons, let happiness seek YOU!

18

As the events in your life evolve into experience, brace yourself for an

incredible day.

Perhaps you will experience inner peace.

Perhaps you will be challenged by success or disappointed by a passing failure.

Perhaps you will be unable to comprehend your contribution to the ocean

of forever;

Perhaps you will be able.

Concentrate on your ability as a positive force to act, reflect, wait, plan, listen

as you light the way for others

to find their path, realize

their hope,...make their contribution.

Share the joy of knowing that the paths exist for each one:

unique, remarkable, purposeful, hopeful.

Wishing to become the person you already are, find the value and joy in

life's present moment.

Life's present is now.

Imagine with resolve. Hope with compassion.

Act without limits.

Light the way for others
to find their path, realize
their hope...make their
contribution to the ocean
of forever.

Looking forward, looking backward, each journey unique...

Challenge yourself to be the meaningful yet infinitely small particle

in the ever-changing river of life.

Without seeing the beginning or ending of this great river, secure your

place in the process,

the flow.

In the river, the journeys overlap, interact, entwine, nurture, affirm, and challenge.

On the journey, everyone receives gifts.

Often the challenges are the gifts...the gifts of growth.

Growth of the wealth inside us:

Life experience

Ongoing perspective

Hopeful purpose

Turning the page to tomorrow,

become present with the moment,

finding that peaceful essence to energize you for the tasks ahead.

Be enhanced by what has been, rather than diminished by what has passed.

Make the life you are choosing also the life you are seeking.

When you reach the other side of tomorrow,

make today the tomorrow you sought.

Open the doors of tomorrow with grace.

Your journey awaits.

...when you reach the other side of tomorrow,

make today the tomorrow you sought.

Just as the seasons change, so must we.

Let us enjoy and be challenged by the seasons

as they give us our examples of change

--our constant.

Seasons become momentary markers in the midst of life's journey.

It is both a shared and a solo journey.

Assigning markers of value along your way,

let the chaos of life define your tranquil nature.

Be creative in your quest for solitude—

a wealth of contentment awaits

the discovery of a tranquil moment.

Be wealthy in contentment and inner peace.

Let memory record magic, not trivia.

Let memory enhance each moment,

each moment unfolding with promise—

unfolding in its own time, not ours—

Promising joy to surpass any sorrows,

and, yes, there will be sorrows.

Live your journey with kind intention,

for kindness is a way of life.

Be both the message and the messenger.

Shine brightly!

...joy to surpass any sorrows, and, yes, there will be sorrows.

Now would be a great time to:

--seek to be responsible and participate to take responsibility.

--expect the best, not because we are entitled,

but because we have given ourselves honorable goals.

--celebrate contrast...the present of the moment.

Seek to identify values and merits,

as we identify the seekers of merits and values.

Expect to determine our commitment

as we commit to our determination.

Celebrate what is ours...

Our values, compassion, goals, energies.

Seek the appropriate ending as we end the inappropriate seeking.

Expect to be stewards of the present

as we accept being beneficiaries of our collective past.

Celebrate the humility that has been delivered to our doorsteps.

Seek solace of knowledge, finding our place in that fine meadow of life

where trust is again a core value.

Expect that our legacy is still to be determined.

Celebrate the comfort in the shadows where we can just begin

to see the joy of light.

Time does not wait...in time, even the mountains will be transient.

Time awaits!

In Joy!

...celebrate contrast,
the present of the moment.

30

Here comes the new day!

How it will be remembered will be a direct result of attitude as

--energies are harnessed

--tasks are defined

--expectations become commitments

--choices become legacy.

The joys of receiving life's blessing are dressed in the masks of tasks...

Fill the horizon with visions of good deeds

--they will follow

--others will follow.

Fill your life as you fill your calendar with

--enough challenges to encourage excellence

--enough experience to navigate wise paths, wisely

--enough pride to be competitive

--enough stamina to reach any finish line, with integrity

--enough appreciation to nurture a peaceful heart

--enough gratitude to overwhelm disappointment

--enough joy

May you find expression for the reverence that
reflects the intrinsic core values of your humanity.

...expectations become commitments

33

How deeply personal is your journey into the future!

Another opportunity awaits in the new day,

its cumulative history brought forth into

your personal portfolio.

Take time to consider what has worked well,

and what has not.

Reconcile what is, with what might be.

Rely on yourself to re-think, re-make, re-assess

and re-evaluate your goals

creating useful measured paths

to facilitate those future endings.

Reward yourself with perspective to understand and

appreciate the magic of an ordinary day.

Respecting yourself, find your sacred place

for the expression of your thoughts,

knowing that there is always one more thought

to add to the landscape of dreams

as well as to the reality of the individual dreamers.

You are here.

Be present.

Presence has its own reward.

Journey on with reverence for the gift of each day,

in awe and with love.

Enjoy.

In Joy.

Journey on with
reverence for
the gift of each day.

Consider that:

Time is life's focusing lens: sorting, sifting, refining, defining.

In foresight, hindsight, insight, we are all seekers.

Questions are the gifts of growth

where actions transform knowledge.

We must fail at succeeding, succeed at failing, before

we can succeed at succeeding.

Choose to:

--become a master of change and adaptation.

--become a survivor of your challenges.

--appreciate the unseen burden of others.

--find contentment in compassion.

--realize that we are not diminished by what we give away.

--seek balance between the noise, the silence, and the song of life.

Know:

Anticipation may envelop fear as well as hope;

may the hope prevail.

In quiet moments, silence speaks.

Listen:

To our future.

Time is life's focusing lens in foresight, hindsight, insight.

What is our harvest at the end of the day?

Be assured:

It is plentiful, bountiful, and beautiful! It is ours.

Be assured:

The new day beckons us all, each to enter with our own joy,

our own purpose, our own mission...

Seek joy in every circumstance.

Be assured:

The new day will be all it is supposed to be, and,

of all possible outcomes,

our energies are an integral part of the good outcomes.

Let it be a magical time of unfolding which we can

anticipate with awe

--and be so pleased.

Let us dismiss worry, for worry will hamper hope.

Let us remember to be kind.

Life not only requires patience, but deserves it.

Be assured:

Our choices and chances for joy await us.

Our harvest, be assured,
is plentiful, bountiful,
beautiful.
It is ours!

42

Responding to life's events,

teaching oneself to respond with Grace,

with Hope,

with Character...

Sounding out the possibilities

the outcomes

the choices

Finding the time,

the concrete, unknown, and finite time,

balanced with the infinite time to which we all belong.

Working to surpass one's own expectations

one thought

one action

one step at a time

Delighting in discovery of

passion, priority, and purpose,

preserving historical perspective

while marching forward to preserve the future,

Remembering that gratitude becomes us all,

the new day beckons.

...remembering that gratitude becomes us all,

as each new day beckons.

Will yourself into a productive future

abandoning "want" and "won't"

as you decide what you WILL do.

Seek and scavenge through the scripts of your life

which you may believe you did not design, envision

or even imagine.

Receive each challenge as an opportunity,

as an intended recipient.

Love this day, its fleeting moments marching past,

returning as memories and markers of our journey.

Love this day, its memories becoming our sense of forever,

memories changing as we change,

becoming anchors going forward.

The soulfulness of life is a patient process,

timelessly bound to the unfolding of individual growth.

Without temptation of delay or assumption of infinity,

begin the journey of good deeds,

outsourcing worries,

harvesting answers from the experience and expertise of others,

as it becomes your experience and proficiency,

as it becomes you,

as it becomes the new day.

...memories changing as we change,
becoming anchors
going forward.

The future is a foreign landscape
full of hopeful dreams and expectations
tethered by present experience.

As experience presents itself
decisions unfold
actions are liberated
energy is expended
as that foreign landscape is cultivated.

Eagerly awaiting the unfolding of our journey

we seek to refine and hone our skills

as well as our hopes.

Writing our future outside the known parameters

--reaching

--learning

--believing

--embracing

--taming that foreign landscape, the new day.

...eagerly awaiting the

unfolding of our journey.

May the blessings of friends and family,

the 'home' we hold dear in our hearts,

give us the comfort and courage to launch

ourselves successfully into a new day.

May your special light illuminate

the lives of those around you, and

lead to insights unsought and

harmonies of which we have not thought.

May your days be productive

and filled with hope.

May your thoughts be blessed

with peaceful understanding

and acceptance of life's mysteries.

...illuminate the lives
of those around you

May your memory of yesterday

be the foundation for today.

May you be blessed with

--the wonder of expectation without fear

--the joy of fulfillment without compromise

--the challenge of the unknown without stress

--the hope of opportunity without loss

May the haven you create

be safe for body and soul.

May the harmony you actively seek be realized.

May the philosophy of life you are unknowingly developing

be worthy of your life's energies.

May paths cross as they are meant to cross

and thoughts transcend time and space boundaries

to give and receive good wishes.

May the opportunities outweigh the obstacles;

may the rewards outnumber the responsibilities;

may the passion for your work and play

be present every day,

not as a means to any end, but to give a

meaningful end to each day.

--may passion for your work and play....

give you a meaningful end to each day.

ON THIS DAY Photography acknowledgements

Sunflower, Sherpa's restaurant, Boulder, Brett Thrash, cover

Uncompahgre National Forest sunrise, Colorado, Jane Thrash, Introduction

Blue Water Carafe, Japango restaurant, Boulder, Brett Thrash, page 3

Sunset, windswept clouds, Pearl Street, Boulder, Brett Thrash, page 6

Ladybugs, Magalloway River Farm, ME, Brett Thrash, page 9

Misty Island, Umbagog National Wildlife Refuge, ME, Brett Thrash, page 12

Balanced Rocks, Sayulita, Nayarit, Mexico, Brett Thrash, page15

Sun Gate at Machu Picchu, Peru, Jane Thrash, page 18

Infinity Pool Moonrise, Le Blanc Spa, Cancun, Mexico, Brett Thrash, page 21

Pawnee Pass Summit, Colorado, Jane Thrash, page 24

White Orchid, Jane Thrash, page 27

Uncompahgre Summit Vista, Colorado, Jane Thrash, page 30

Seagulls, Cancun Mexico, Brett Thrash, page 33

Sunrise through Airplane Window, Denver International Airport, Brett Thrash, page 36

Sunset through Rearview Mirror, Eisenhower Tunnel, Colorado, Brett Thrash, page 39

Sunflower, Sherpa's restaurant, Boulder, Brett Thrash, page 42

Misty Morning Sunrise Reflection, Umbagog National Wildlife Refuge, Brett Thrash, page 45

Jar of Sand, Jane Thrash, page 48

View from Plane, Shadow approaching Boat, Caribbean Sea, Brett Thrash, page 51

Afternoon Sun, Sayulita, Nayarit, Mexico, Brett Thrash, page 54

Winter Sunset Reflection, Arapahoe Road, Boulder, Brett Thrash, page 57

Royal Arch, Boulder, Jane Thrash, closing photo, page 59

Acknowledgements

Special thanks to Melanie Nygren whose friendship began as my fellow student at the University of Colorado Boulder and continued as my employer and forever friend, always challenging me to find, explore, and develop my unique value.

Thanks also to my childhood friend Vicki Roark whose adult friendship has become sisterhood by choice.

Thanks to Rachel Weaver of the Louisville Writer's Workshop whose calm instructive words have helped me to find and accept my voice.

Thanks to Kerrie Flanagan Director of the Northern Colorado Writers Association who has helped me navigate the waters of publication to realize the completion of this book.

Thanks to Marla Rutherford of Marla Rutherford Photography for the author photograph.

Thanks to my mother Virginia who continues to inspire so many as she charts new paths, on her daily mission to make people smile.

Thanks to my son Brett, truly the "wind beneath my wings."

About the Author

Jane Thrash was born in St. Louis, Missouri, raised in Oklahoma, and grew up in Colorado where she has resided since 1970. She attended the University of Colorado Boulder as an adult student receiving a Bachelor's Degree in Journalism and Public Relations. She has one son, Brett, who gave purpose to her life, and whose friendship and wit she cherishes. Writing, gardening, and fitness are pillars of her activities, and harmony of presence is her goal. Through decades of work in real estate and mortgage financing, her love of words sustained her, and continues.

CPSIA information can be obtained at www.ICGtesting.com
Printed in the USA
LVIW01n0412241015
459117LV00003B/4